Usborne Workbooks
Multiplying

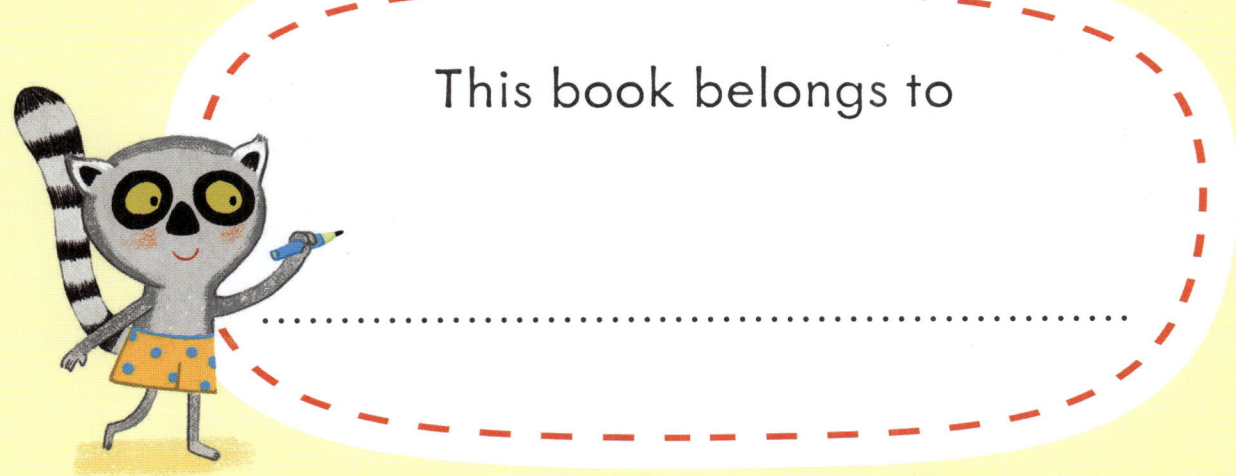

This book belongs to

....

There are answers on page 27, and notes
for grown-ups at the back of the book.

Here are some of the animals you'll meet in this book. Use a pen or pencil to trace over the numbers on their cards.

Cheeky

1
one
●

Lep

2
two
● ●

Ant

3
three
● ● ●

Tig

4
four
● ● ● ●

Baz

5
five
● ● ● ● ●

Crock

6
six
● ● ● ● ● ●

Help the animals with their calculations in this book.
Draw over the dotted lines and write the numbers in the boxes.

Usborne Workbooks
Multiplying

Illustrated by Marta Cabrol

Written by Holly Bathie
Designed by Meg Dobbie
and Keith Newell

Froggy

seven

Lem

eight

Beaky

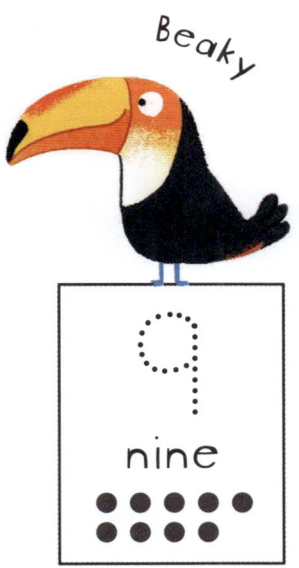

nine

Tan-tan

ten

At the end of
the book there are
blank pages for more
multiplying practice.

Edited by Jessica Greenwell
and Kristie Pickersgill
Series Editor: Felicity Brooks

Two by two

Help Baz count each shoe in the jungle store.
Write how many there are after each pair.

There are ☐ shelves and ☐ shoes on each shelf.

There are ☐ shoes altogether.

Help Cheeky continue counting in 2s along the shelves.

Cheeky

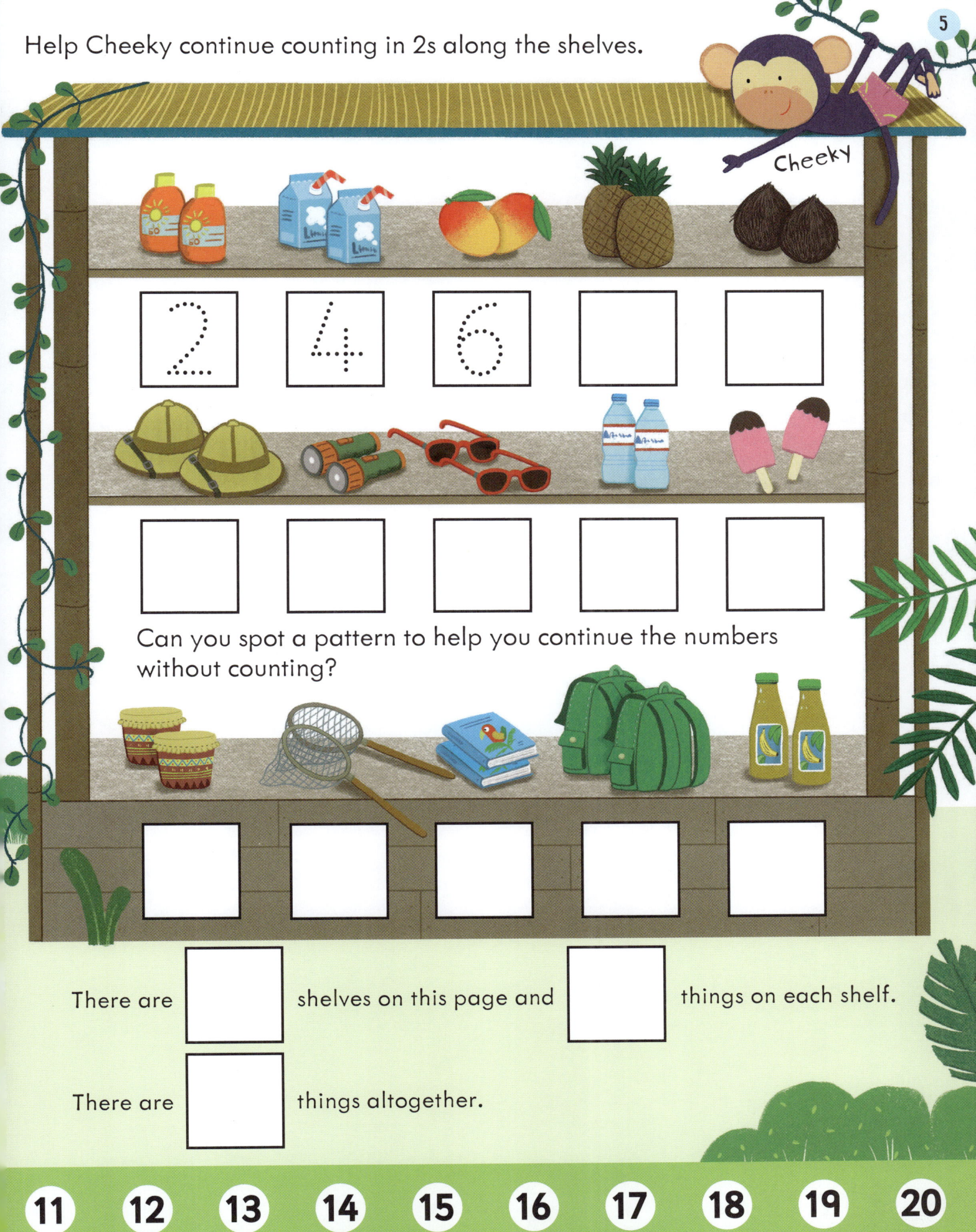

| 2 | 4 | 6 | | |

Can you spot a pattern to help you continue the numbers without counting?

There are ☐ shelves on this page and ☐ things on each shelf.

There are ☐ things altogether.

11 12 13 14 15 16 17 18 19 20

Number patterns

Cheeky is collecting bananas in bunches of 3 and counting how many she will have altogether after each bunch. Trace the numbers along her path and continue her counting.

3   6

Baz has 5 toes on each foot. Trace the numbers along his muddy trail and write how many toe prints there are altogether after each footprint.

5   10

1   2   3   4   5   6   7   8   9   10

If you can see a pattern in this trail of 5s, try writing the rest of the numbers without counting.

11 12 13 14 15 16 17 18 19 20

Groups of 10

It's the family boat race today. There are 2 boats at the front, each with 10 animals in. Write how many animals there are altogether.

Cheeky   Cheeky's family

Lep   Lep's family

We're so close!

| 2 | boats of | 10 | animals | = | | animals |

1 more boat of 10 animals is catching up. Write how many animals there are now.

Ant   Ant's family

| 3 | boats of | 10 | animals | = | | animals |

1 more boat of 10 animals is behind. Fill in the boxes to show how many boats there are now, and how many animals altogether.

Keep going!

Baz

Baz's family

☐ boats of **10** animals = ☐ animals

If 10 more animals joined, in 1 more boat, how many boats would there be, and how many animals altogether? Fill in the boxes.

☐ boats of **10** animals = ☐ animals

If another 10 animals joined, in 1 more boat, how many boats would there be, and how many animals altogether? Fill in the boxes.

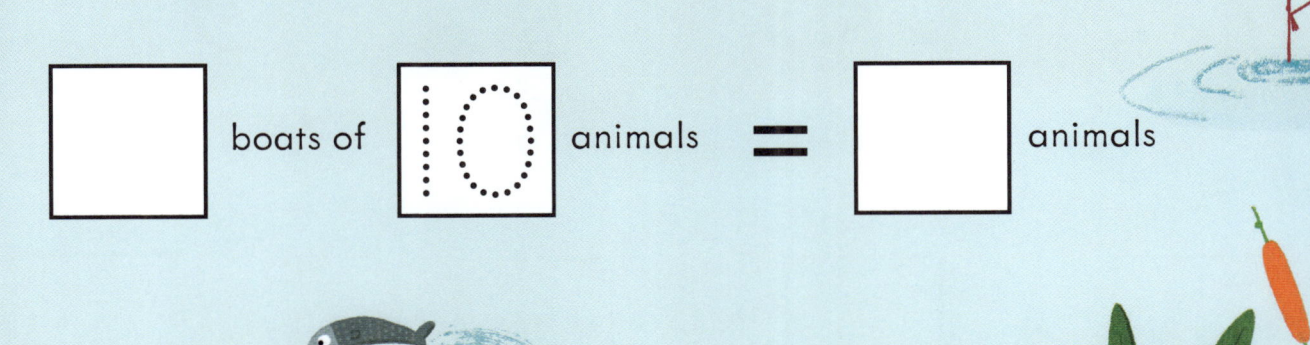

☐ boats of **10** animals = ☐ animals

Three numbers the same

The animals are having a dance competition and the scores are in. Copy the scores into the boxes and write the total score for each couple.

Ten   Ten   Ten

10   10   10

☐ + ☐ + ☐ =

TOTAL SCORE ☐

Three 10s

Five   Five   Five

5   5   5

☐ + ☐ + ☐ =

TOTAL SCORE ☐

Three 5s

$\square$ + $\square$ + $\square$ = TOTAL SCORE $\square$

Three 3s

$\square$ + $\square$ + $\square$ = TOTAL SCORE $\square$

Three 2s

Draw a star next to the couple that has won the dance trophy.

Groups of parrots

The parrots are sitting in groups of 2. Complete the adding calculation to show how many parrots there are altogether.

☐ + ☐ + ☐ = ☐ parrots

Three 2s

When you are adding groups of the same number you can use the 'multiplying' sign. It's also called the 'times' sign. Beaky is pointing to it.

X

Squawk!

The parrots have moved into different groups. Can you complete the new calculation?

 2 X ☐ groups of = 6 parrots

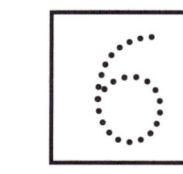

The parrots have moved into 1 big group.
Complete this calculation.

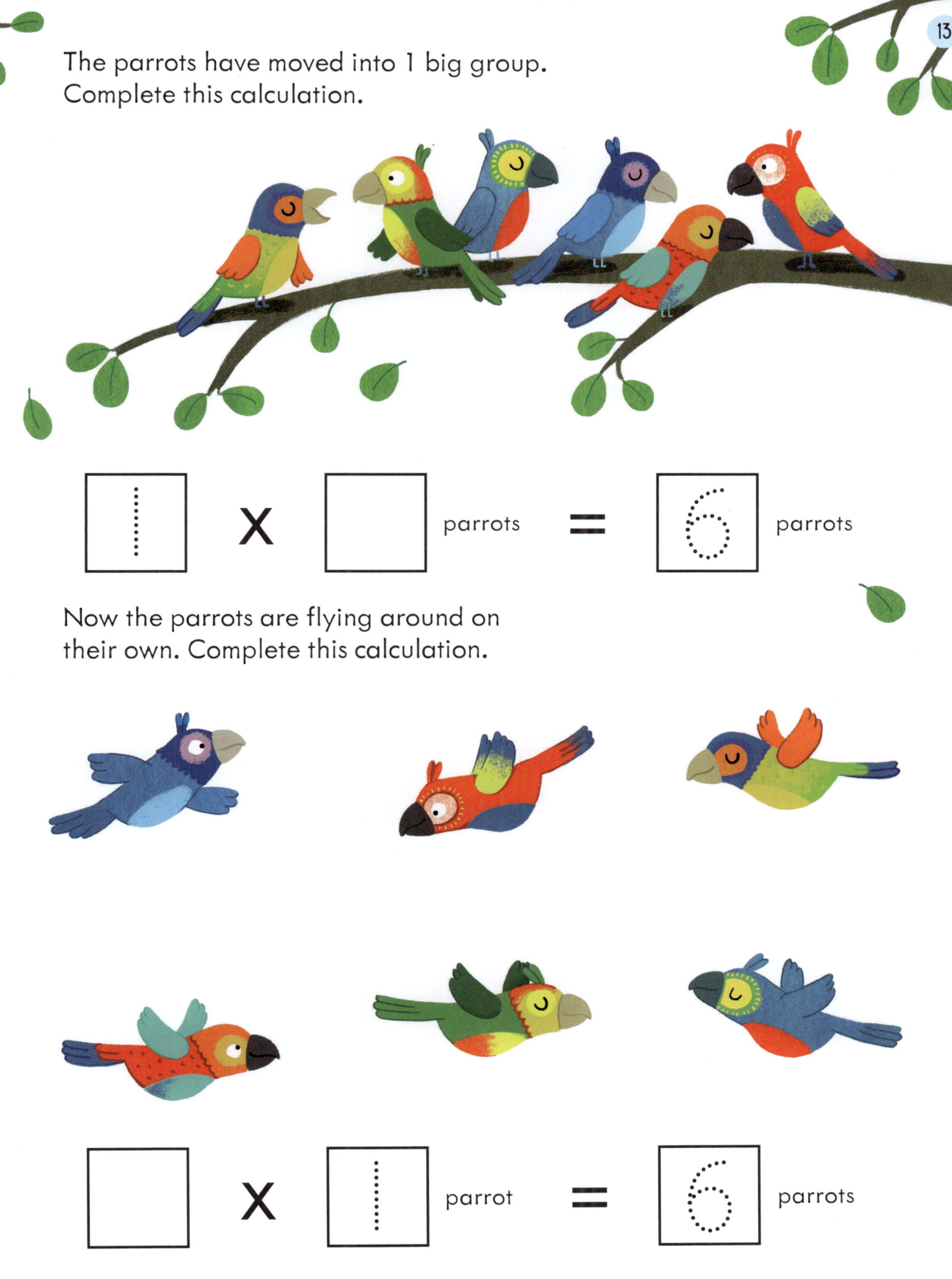

| 1 | X | | parrots | = | 6 | parrots |

Now the parrots are flying around on their own. Complete this calculation.

| | X | 1 | parrot | = | 6 | parrots |

Making groups

Help Ant work out how many butterflies there are in the set below.
Draw a ring around a group of 4 butterflies. Keep drawing rings
around groups of 4 until all the butterflies are in groups.

Write how many groups you have made to complete the calculation.

☐ groups of **X** 4 butterflies **=** 20 butterflies

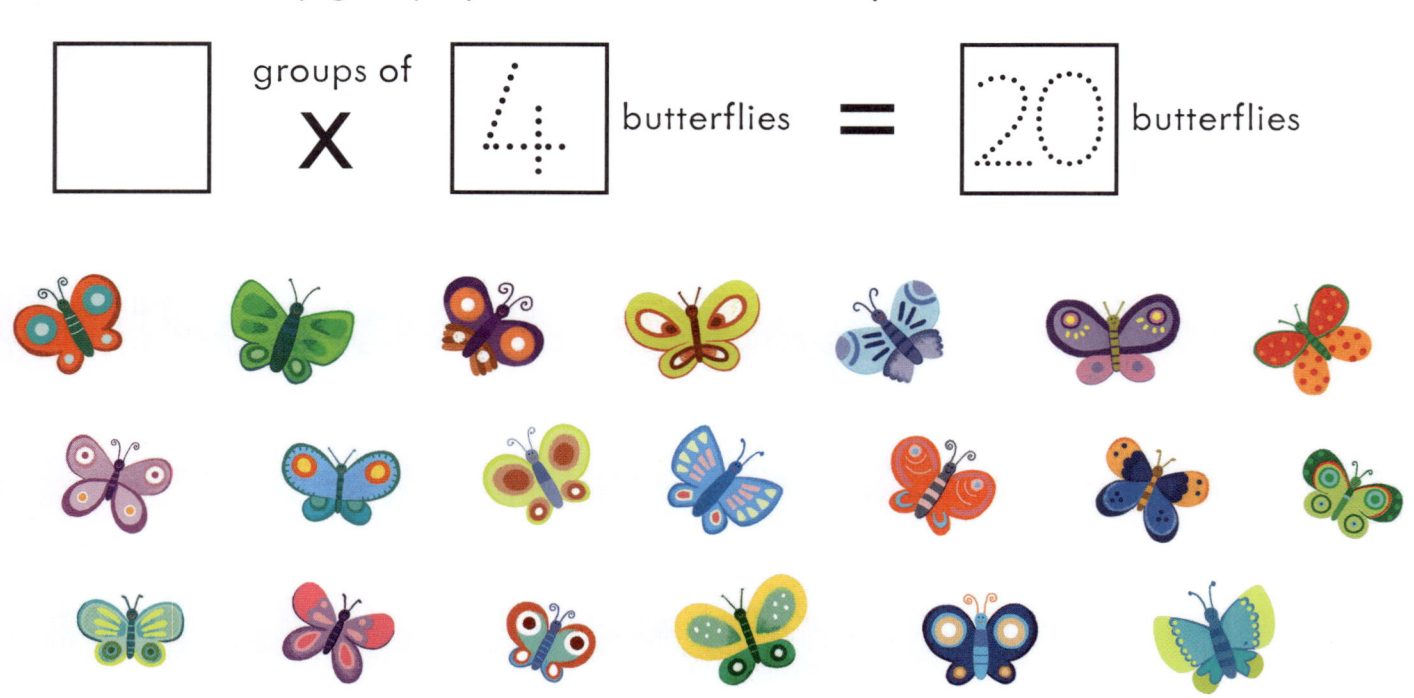

Now count the butterflies in groups of 5. Draw rings around
groups of 5 butterflies and then complete the calculation.

 **X** 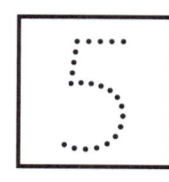 butterflies **=**  butterflies

Now count the butterflies in groups of 10. Draw rings around groups of 10 butterflies and then complete the calculation.

☐ X 10 butterflies = 20 butterflies

Complete the calculations below to show other ways of grouping the butterflies. You could draw and group butterflies on the blank pages at the back of the book, to help you work out the answers.

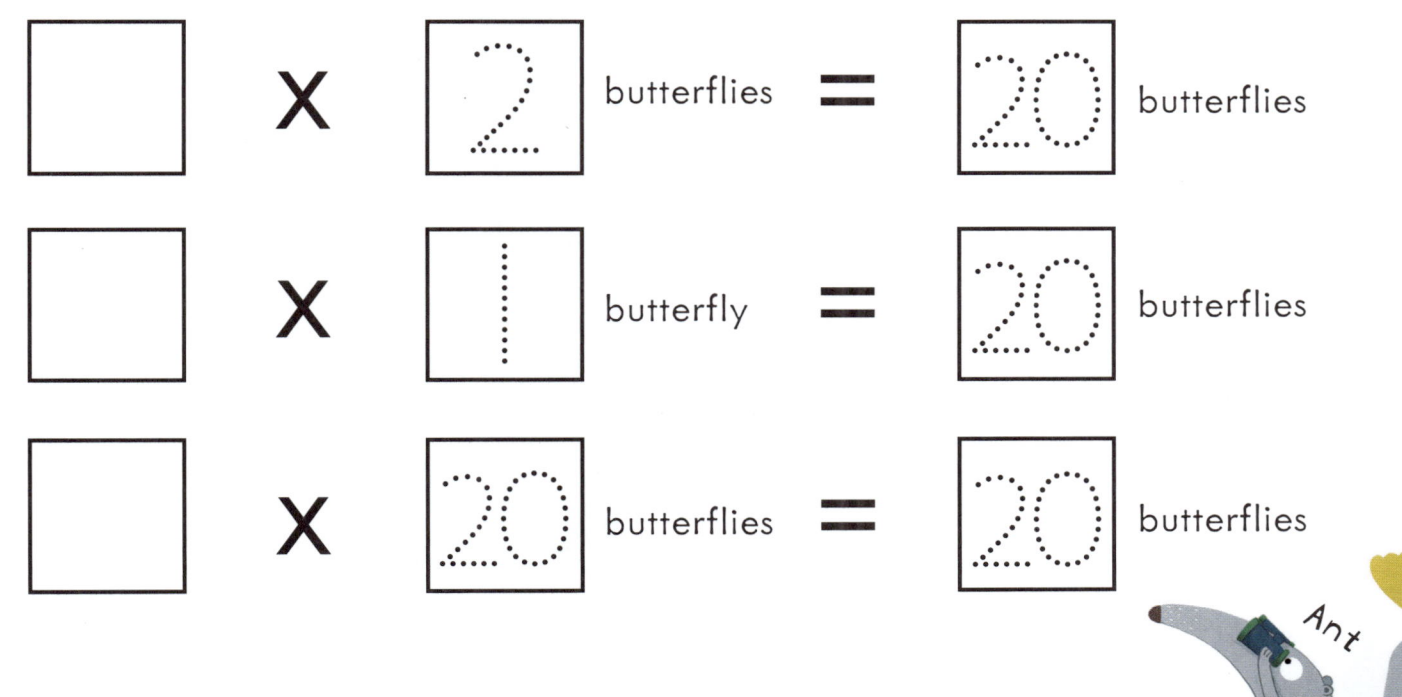

☐ X 2 butterflies = 20 butterflies

☐ X 1 butterfly = 20 butterflies

☐ X 20 butterflies = 20 butterflies

Ant

More multiplying

The animals are playing in the jungle. How many spots are there on these leopards? Complete the calculation.

$$4 \quad \times \quad \boxed{} \text{ spots} \quad = \quad \boxed{} \text{ spots}$$

How many monkey ears are there in total below? Complete the calculation.

$$\boxed{} \quad \times \quad 2 \text{ ears} \quad = \quad \boxed{} \text{ ears}$$

Help the animals with their
multiplying calculations.

5 x 10 =

6 x 3 =

2 x 4 =

10 x 5 =

5 x 3 =

3 x 3 =

I think I know
the answer.

This
is fun!

Spotting patterns

1	2	3	4	5	6	7	8	9	10
11	12	13	14	15	16	17	18	19	20
21	22	23	24	25	26	27	28	29	30
31	32	33	34	35	36	37	38	39	40
41	42	43	44	45	46	47	48	49	50
51	52	53	54	55	56	57	58	59	60
61	62	63	64	65	66	67	68	69	70
71	72	73	74	75	76	77	78	79	80
81	82	83	84	85	86	87	88	89	90
91	92	93	94	95	96	97	98	99	100

The animals are looking for patterns in the number grid. Help them to draw the patterns.

Draw a circle around each of the numbers in the 2s pattern for me.

It starts 2, 4, 6, 8, 10...

Lep

Draw a triangle around each of the numbers in the 5s pattern for me.

It starts 5, 10, 15, 20, 25...

Lem

Look, Tan-tan, the numbers that are in a triangle AND a circle make a new pattern.

Crock

Tan-tan

Oh yes! The new pattern is the pattern of...

Write the answer in the box for me.

Multiplying with 2 and 3

Cheeky and Tig are doing more pattern spotting. Can you see which patterns they have drawn?

1	②△	③	④	5	⑥△	7	⑧	△9	⑩
11	⑫△	13	⑭	△15	⑯	17	⑱△	19	⑳
△21	㉒	23	㉔△	25	㉖	㉗△	㉘	29	㉚△
31	32	33	34	35	36	37	38	39	40
41	42	43	44	45	46	47	48	49	50

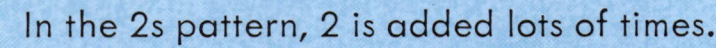

In the 2s pattern, 2 is added lots of times. The numbers in this pattern are 'multiples' of 2.

In the 3s pattern, 3 is added lots of times. The numbers in this pattern are 'multiples' of 3.

Squawk!

I've drawn a circle around the multiples of 2. Finish the pattern for me.

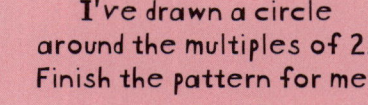

I've drawn a triangle around the multiples of 3. Finish the pattern for me.

12 has a circle AND a triangle around it.
This means it is a multiple of both 2 and 3.

Cheeky has counted to 12 in multiples of 2.
Trace the numbers in her multiplying calculation.

$6 \times 2 =$ ☐

I counted 2 six times
to get to 12.
Six lots of 2 is 12.

Tig has counted to 12 in multiples of 3.
Trace the numbers in his multiplying calculation.

$4 \times 3 =$ ☐

I counted 3 four times
to get to 12.
Four lots of 3 is 12.

Look for the next number after 12 in the grid that is a multiple
of 2 and 3, and write it in both of the blue boxes below.

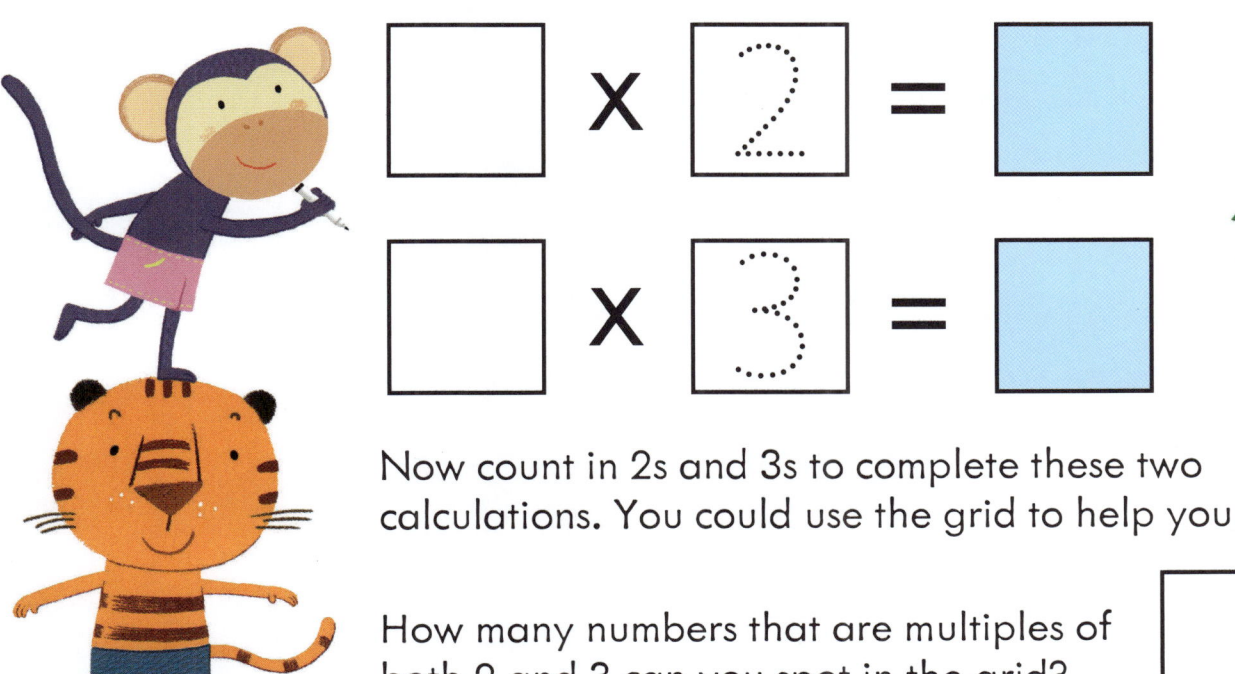

$☐ \times 2 = $ ☐

$☐ \times 3 = $ ☐

Now count in 2s and 3s to complete these two
calculations. You could use the grid to help you.

How many numbers that are multiples of
both 2 and 3 can you spot in the grid?

☐

Sorting multiples

These football players need to get into their teams. Write each player's number under the right team name on the next page.

You could cross out each number on this page as you go.

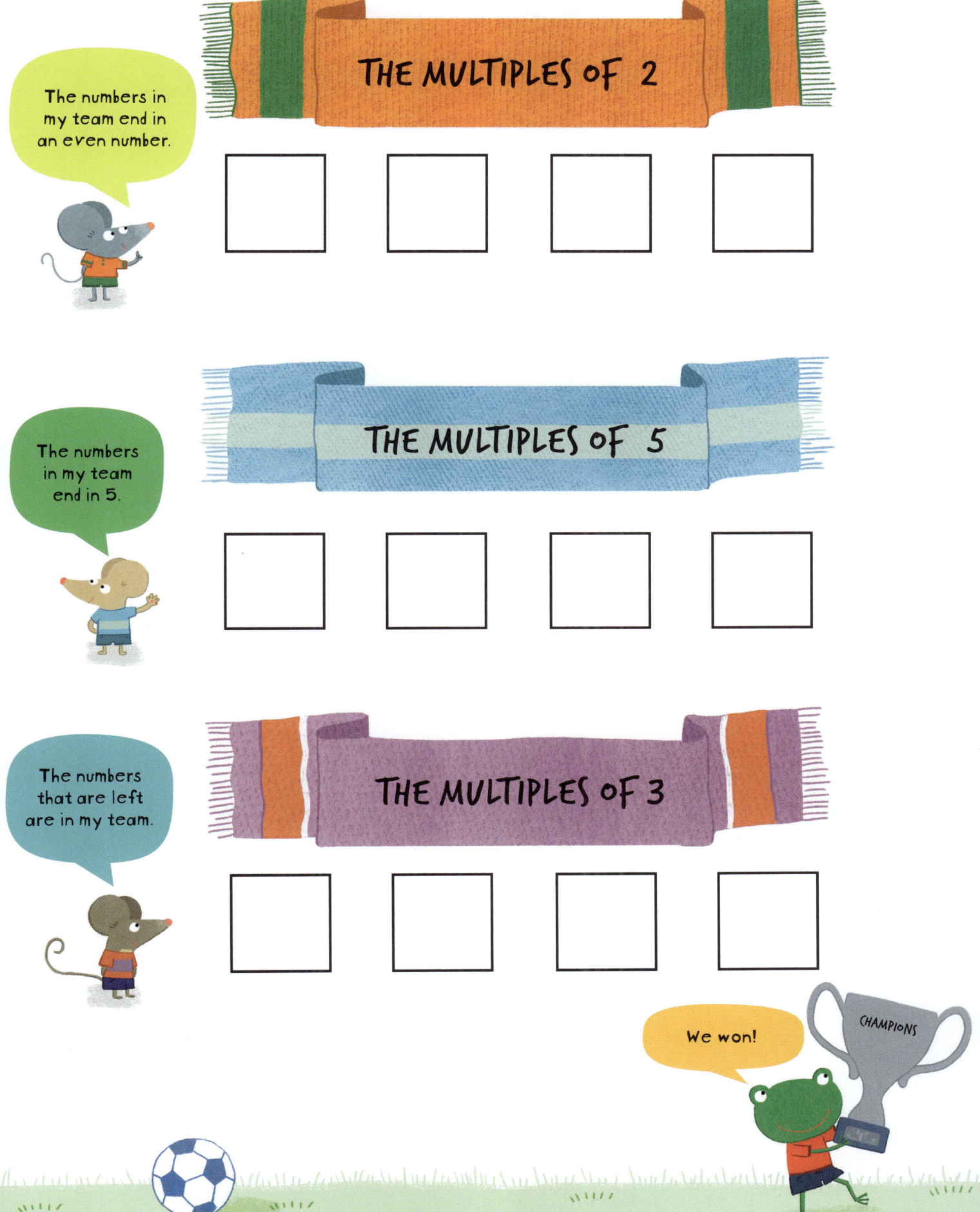

Multiplying quiz

Find out how much you can remember about
multiplying by doing this quiz. Answers on page 26.

A. Ant, Lep and Beaky have forgotten some of the numbers in their
    patterns. Write the missing numbers in the boxes for them.

Mine is the 2s
pattern.

34   36   ☐   40   42   44   ☐

Mine is the 5s
pattern.

15   20   25   ☐   35   40   ☐

Mine is the 3s
pattern.

9   12   15   18   ☐   24   ☐

B. The animals are adding in their heads to work out how much food they have collected. Show them how they could multiply instead to find the answer – write a multiplying calculation for each animal.

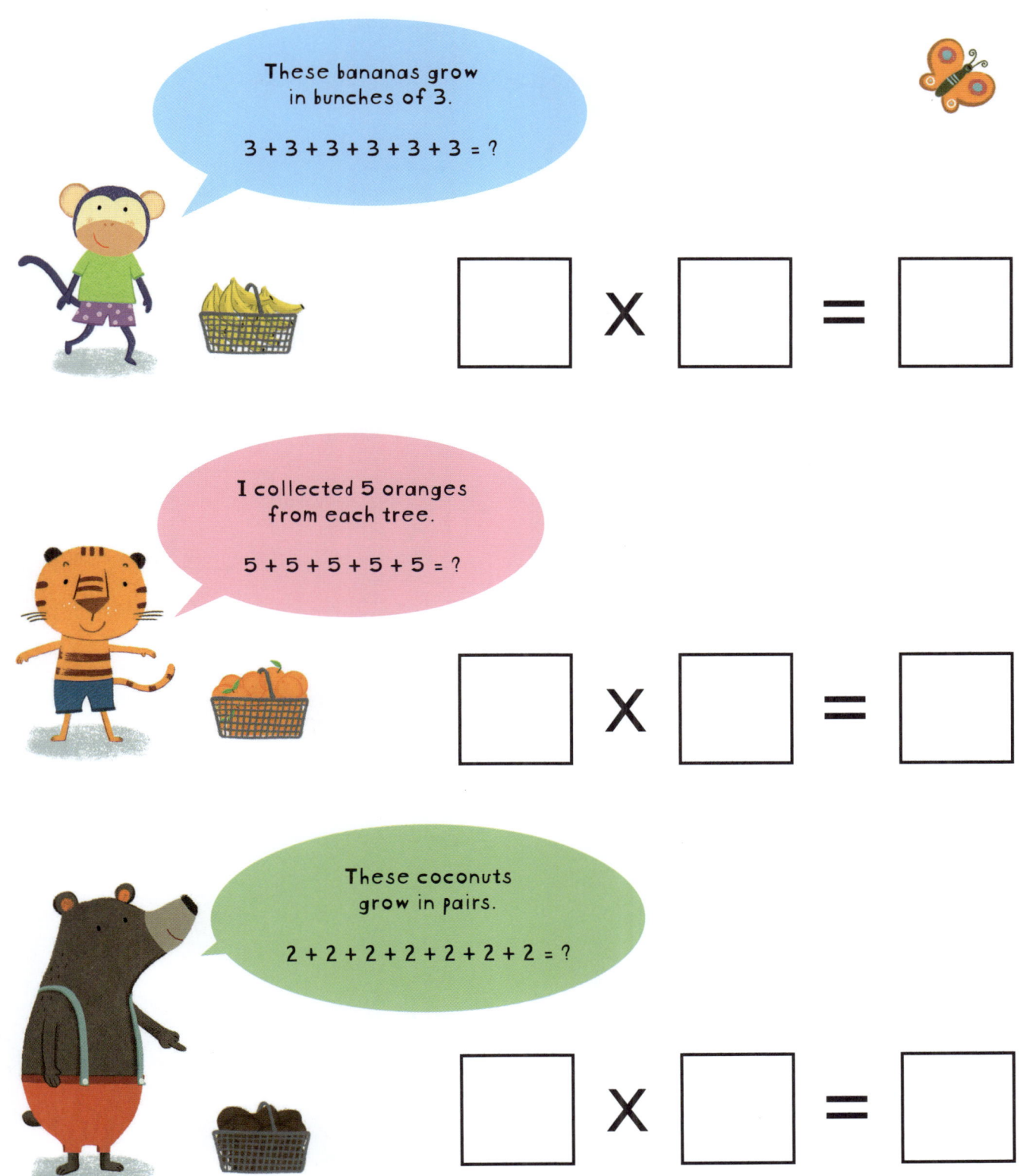

These bananas grow in bunches of 3.

3 + 3 + 3 + 3 + 3 + 3 = ?

☐ X ☐ = ☐

I collected 5 oranges from each tree.

5 + 5 + 5 + 5 + 5 = ?

☐ X ☐ = ☐

These coconuts grow in pairs.

2 + 2 + 2 + 2 + 2 + 2 + 2 = ?

☐ X ☐ = ☐

C. Complete these calculations for Tan-tan and Crock.

9 x 5 = ☐   7 x 3 = ☐   8 x 3 = ☐

3 x 2 = ☐   5 x 8 = ☐   6 x 2 = ☐

2 x 9 = ☐   2 x 8 = ☐   3 x 3 = ☐

5 x 4 = ☐   3 x 5 = ☐   7 x 5 = ☐

10 x 5 = ☐   10 x 2 = ☐

Quiz answers

A. 34   36   [38]   40   42   44   [46]   B.   6 x 3 = 18

    15   20   25   [30]   35   40   [45]   5 x 5 = 25

     9   12   15   18   [21]   24   [27]   7 x 2 = 14

C. 9 x 5 = 45   7 x 3 = 21   8 x 3 = 24   10 x 5 = 50

    3 x 2 = 6   5 x 8 = 40   6 x 2 = 12   10 x 2 = 20

    2 x 9 = 18   2 x 8 = 16   3 x 3 = 9

    5 x 4 = 20   3 x 5 = 15   7 x 5 = 35

Score 1 point for each correct answer and write your score in this box: ☐ 23

Answers

pages 4-5

2, 4, 6, 8, 10
12, 14, 16, 18, 20
There are 2 shelves and 10 shoes on each shelf. There are 20 shoes altogether.

2, 4, 6, 8, 10
12, 14, 16, 18, 20
22, 24, 26, 28, 30
There are 3 shelves and 10 things on each shelf. There are 30 things altogether.

pages 6-7

3, 6, 9, 12, 15, 18
5, 10, 15, 20, 25, 30, 35

pages 8-9

2 groups of 10 animals = 20 animals
3 groups of 10 animals = 30 animals
4 groups of 10 animals = 40 animals
5 groups of 10 animals = 50 animals
6 groups of 10 animals = 60 animals

pages 10-11

$10 + 10 + 10 = 30$ ★
$5 + 5 + 5 = 15$
$3 + 3 + 3 = 9$
$2 + 2 + 2 = 6$

pages 12-13

$2 + 2 + 2 = 6$ (or $3 \times 2 = 6$)
$2 \times 3 = 6$
$1 \times 6 = 6$
$6 \times 1 = 6$

pages 14-15

$5 \times 4 = 20$ $10 \times 2 = 20$
$4 \times 5 = 20$ $20 \times 1 = 20$
$2 \times 10 = 20$ $1 \times 20 = 20$

pages 16-17

$4 \times 10 = 40$ $2 \times 4 = 8$
$10 \times 2 = 20$ $10 \times 5 = 50$
$5 \times 10 = 50$ $5 \times 3 = 15$
$6 \times 3 = 18$ $3 \times 3 = 9$

pages 18-19

1	2	3	4	5	6	7	8	9	10
11	12	13	14	15	16	17	18	19	20
21	22	23	24	25	26	27	28	29	30
31	32	33	34	35	36	37	38	39	40
41	42	43	44	45	46	47	48	49	50
51	52	53	54	55	56	57	58	59	60
61	62	63	64	65	66	67	68	69	70
71	72	73	74	75	76	77	78	79	80
81	82	83	84	85	86	87	88	89	90
91	92	93	94	95	96	97	98	99	100

The third pattern is the 10s pattern. Numbers that are multiples of both 2 and 5 are also multiples of 10.

pages 20-21

$6 \times 2 = 12$ $9 \times 2 = 18$
$4 \times 3 = 12$ $6 \times 3 = 18$

There are 8 multiples of both 2 and 3 in the grid.

pages 22-23

Multiples of 2: 22, 38, 52, 64
Multiples of 5: 25, 35, 75, 95
Multiples of 3: 21, 57, 69, 93

You can use these pages for more multiplying practice.

30

Notes for grown-ups

Two by two (pages 4-5)
Once children have counted in 2s to 20, they may be able to spot the repeating pattern of '2, 4, 6, 8, 10' to help them to write the next row of numbers without counting. They may realize that the number of shoes is double the number of pairs.

Number patterns (pages 6-7)
This activity gives children the opportunity to count in 3s and 5s, and to see that the numbers in the 5s pattern end in '5' or '0' alternately.

Groups of 10 (pages 8-9)
This encourages children to practise adding '10 more' using the language of 'lots of' or 'groups of' 10.

Three numbers the same (pages 10-11)
In this activity children can practise repeated adding of the same number and link that to their learning of the 2s, 3s, 5s and 10s patterns. Discuss with children that, for example, 'three 5s' means 'three groups of 5' or '5, 10, 15'.

Groups of parrots (pages 12-13)
This activity introduces the 'X' sign to represent 'groups of' the same number in a calculation. These pages show the different ways 6 parrots can be put into groups of the same number. This is why the numbers in a multiplying calculation can be written in any order and the total won't change.

Making groups (pages 14-15)
Children can practise making their own groups to check that however an amount is grouped, the total amount always remains the same.

More multiplying (pages 16-17)
Here children have the opportunity to practise recalling some of the multiplying facts they have learned.

Spotting patterns (pages 18-19)
This activity shows children that some numbers appear in more than one pattern, so they are multiples of more than one number. Children may be able to spot other patterns, for example: all even numbers are multiples of 2, and multiples of 3 and 5 alternate between odd and even numbers.

Multiplying with 2 and 3 (pages 20-21)
This activity allows children to find numbers that are multiples of both 2 and 3 and write their own multiplication calculations about them.

Sorting multiples (pages 22-23)
Here children have the opportunity to identify and sort multiples of 2, 3 and 5. If they are stuck, suggest they start by finishing the multiples of 2 and 5 first.